SHADOWS BURNING

· *W. S. Di Piero* ·

SHADOWS

BURNING

TRIQUARTERLY BOOKS
NORTHWESTERN UNIVERSITY PRESS

Evanston, Illinois

TriQuarterly Books

Northwestern University Press

Evanston, Illinois 60208-4210

Copyright © 1995 by W. S. Di Piero

All rights reserved

Printed in the United States of America

ISBN   cloth 0-8101-5019-0

          paper 0-8101-5020-4

Library of Congress Cataloging-in-Publication Data

Di Piero, W. S.

    Shadows burning.

        p.   cm.

    ISBN 0-8101-5019-0 (cloth). — ISBN 0-8101-5020-4

    (paper)

    PS3554.I65S48   1995

    811'.54—dc20   95-35349

                                            CIP

Still, one loves America above all things, for her youth, her greenness, her plasticity, innocence, good intentions, friends, everything.

WILLIAM JAMES

The effort really to see and really to represent is no idle business in the face of the constant force that makes for muddlement.

HENRY JAMES

CONTENTS

· III ·

ACKNOWLEDGMENTS

Grateful acknowledgments are made to the following magazines in which some of the poems in this volume first appeared:

The New Criterion
"Red Roses"

The New Yorker
"California Thrasher"

Pequod
"22nd Street"

Poetry
"On a Picture by Cézanne"

Southern Review
"Far West"

The Threepenny Review
"The Sleepers," "In the Driveway," "The Depot"

TriQuarterly
"Karloff and the Rock," "The Mummers," "Reading Ovid," "Shrine with Flowers," "Saturday Afternoon," "Buddy's Corner," "Self-Portrait"

Yale Review
"Windy Hill"

· I ·

pacific

Shrine with Flowers

FOR MARY JANE

1

She squeezes sideways
through the screen door,
the small knobby apples
slung in her apron
bump her knees and thighs,
five years of drought
but a sort of harvest,
a gift at least, anyway
I feel it to be so
when her hands open,
the fruit crashing
into the sink,
and her apron disappears.

2

After the chemo sessions,
my neighbor's wife retreats
to bed and fear,
while across the fence
he and I talk above
a vagrant cavernous smell
of old camphor leaves.
But he is fingering
the plum tree graft
where years ago he sheathed
new bud into old stock,
wedded, barked over,
toughened every season.
We'll have fruit, real sweet,
he says, grinding his thumb
at the splice. Really
good dark black purple.

3

It's all haywire,
(her old letter still
sweating in my pocket
as I double dig a patch
as per her command)
your heart. Can't you
stop working, or "work"
at knowing yourself?
You act as if acting
matters. Just stop.
Can't you let yourself
not do, for a change?
House finches doubling
down to a branch
mating for life
while the grinding
orange poppies open
through the rusting
chainlink fence that
defines this ditch.

4

A sunny wind,

her eyelash

scraping my cheek.

And familiar words

housed in her breath.

Habit and talk,

rose petals, ice,

scent of apples,

laughter tilted back

in her mouth,

even when she

comes back after

visiting next door.

What do we hold

so loosely in common?

Crows in the seedy patch.

Treetops moved by the wind.

The shivering tips of grass.

5

Cautious, with their dainty wrestler's walk, the raccoons came for Nick's corn. They also tore up some lettuce and beans. (One found pet rabbits three houses down, lifted the latch and climbed inside the cage, crouching a while there before he killed.) So he designed and built wood steelmesh traps. The coons mocked the prototype, they stole the bait, sprung the trapdoor and ran free, then tore up more garden and knocked over the garbage. The revised design worked. While Luisa kept records of her painkillers and watched T.V., bored to panic by soaps and game shows and all that scripted hilarity and dismay, Nick transported the trapped raccoons fifteen miles up into the redwoods above the skyline road where the hills start to slope down to the ocean. This way, he says, they won't come back, you don't have to kill them.

6

Roses on the table,
how many days, drooping
late March red roses
left out too long
for our small pleasure.
Smelling of old beer,
like my first house,
the blurred men home
late from the taproom,
who pitched like shades
across the T.V. screen,
blue men, blue vase,
this cloudware cube
painted with vague
welkin roses, phantom
blooms that last longer,
rising toward the real
flopped red petals,
my father's pockets
turned inside out.

7

"What's for dinner?" she asks.
Coon tails and tofu tiramisù
alla california. No kidding.
So we tend our cakey garden
another hour, pulling weeds
we overspent our water rations
to prime last spring. A chilly
fall evening, a shorter day.
The cosmos are blaring.
We sample peppery nasturtiums
that melt on the tongue,
while morning glories
snarl the chainlink.
Why didn't we think
to plant cucumbers and squash,
or entreat the house finches
to bring us cantaloupe?
Why dig and kill our backs
to cultivate these gauds
so unlike our own flesh?

8

Clearing green trash in the backyard, I thought I'd go next door and say something to Luisa, anything, knowing that if I had to I'd just push words around, to testify or console, make small talk, make a sentence. The camphor leaves I grabbed behind the bird-of-paradise—a rain mould pitted the alarmed spiky flowers—crumbled in my gloves. The leaves were papery and dim, but that chilly odor broke from them, and then I'm in bed with pneumonia, studying the Blue Book reports on UFOs, Sid Caesar purses his lips before station break, somewhere in the house my father is bashfully drunk. Language is falling into senselessness like leaves. It has always felt like accidents of meaning, I'm recalling, the world made over in a casual coincidence of noises that are words. I held them in my crummy gloves, two seasons' leaves from the camphor trees, Luisa's cancer treatments overlapping them. Now she's getting radiation for the pain, fusses over the wig she never wears around the house, and keeps her walker close, though most days I hear her lovely clear voice hollering out the back door: "Nick, what are you doing now?" I spent a week trying to control the blackberry. ("Do you ever hear yourself? *Control.*") It shot up and climbed across the pavement, up and through the chainlink, then into the rotten shed, prising under its boards and ribs and around the skinny plum trees. Blackberries so sweet after a rainy season that they hurt your teeth and make children tear their arms and faces on brambles to get at the fruit so that they can eat themselves sick.

9

"Takes one to know one,"
she says, while the wind
grazing our bare backs
lifts the roses' scent
and blows it through weeds
we're pulling like mad.
Then the grass shifts
direction, tree shadows
jerk across the house,
rose blooms knock heads.
We're looking for something,
but what? Shadow of what?
"Gone with the wind, kiddo."

10

Tonight the grass gets
a dusting sort of rain
that reminds me of drought.
One night last winter, I walked
near the Schuylkill oilworks;
the ghoulish streetlights dusted
the shaggy boys I heard
—"Give it up, asshole!"—
before I saw them shuffling
under the schoolyard hoop.
Their gray moonlight, tossed
shades mixed with darkness,
comes back to me now,
sheeting my field of view
where sluggy, sun-logged, brief
Pacific greens wait
for winter, chilled by shadows
burnt and burning cold.

11

Luisa, Italian beauty, emigrant
Canada to California (wife of Nicola,
union carpenter, called Marchigiani,
of the Marches, emigrant 1950),
attached to the morphine drip
and catheter, in her conscious hours
wants this room where she will die
spotless, tidy as the garden
where the last sweet chard grows.
The mute T.V. wipes from face
to gunfire to White House lawn.
Nick talks over the pied images
to himself, stands to greet neighbors
who sit an hour or so with her.
Twice he reminds me to take
whatever fruit I find out back.
A few apricots past their prime.
The first figs, mostly green
or purply blue like vein made flesh.
A few hard young mossy peaches,
plus leathery pomegranates,
their seeds forcing through the seams
as we force into her bright room
crowding at her side to wait.

12

The breeze, our bedroom window,
the dark, and her breath
tiding at my ear.
The leaves of the plant
whose name I haven't learned
stirring at that sound,
the pitched lift and fall,
while the moon's dense light
pebbles through the leaves
onto her pillow and face,
writing the motion, unselfed.
Wake and tell me, tell me.

Far West

Lilac I never saw
by Watkins Street's housefronts,
diestamped windows, brick,
the sphinx of granite steps
I rubbed my face against.
Smells of roofpitch, dust,
burnt peppers. Telephone-
trees, pavements edged
with moss worms, Death Box
chalked on hot blacktop.
Lilac I knew only
in satin color plates
in libraries, and once
in flesh at Bartram's Garden,
where sullen, square, pouchy
Gumbo the Calabrese
drove me from the city
into a late spring twilight,
pointing (*Smell? There?*)
to flowers he would not name,
until his choppy English
made this: *Are lilacs!*

Now two weeks' chilled
sagging mist grinds
our Pacific mornings,
and it comes to me,
so unlikely, unreal
this far west, it has
its legend, the bland
bluesmoke ceanothus,
"called California lilac."
But what comes to me
is Gumbo Bartram's bloom,
barely surviving, throbbing
where there's no right time,
no hard freeze or winter
sleep. In the broken time
I work this out in lines,
in the patch of green behind
this house I do not own,
real lilacs bloom, turn
my head, and go. Leaving,
they are so much with me
that I'm never home again.

California Thrasher

Dirt grenades blown around
his big head, he labors
under the lemon tree,
blossom and fruit, bright leaves,
he trenches the dirt,
he hammers, he feeds, down
where earth's muscled rind wraps
around its molten core,
sea of blue mud flames,
combed fire, swell, cooling foam,
where our dead are waiting,
where we await ourselves,
he works, hungry, fearless,
our only messenger.

In the Driveway

FOR P.K.

When all five tumble from the wingsprung doors
the instant you hit the brakes, I see Julian,
younger then, goofy, hoarse with fear and joy,
flapping from the handle like a last leaf
while your husband laughed, gunned the engine,
shouting at him to be a man, hold on,
or shut the goddamn door. He's the first one out.

I never remember the girls' names.
Laura's Number One, Emma's Two, like that,
until I stammer and lose count at Four.
Mashing giggles, they trip across the gravel.
As usual, you're off to the side, dressy,
trembling, sunny floral skirt ticking.
Your shepherding look holds nothing back.

What words held you those smeared, blissy nights
you drank together, his gun under the pillow
or at your head when he choked you awake?
The children slamming cardoors, one cocked ajar . . .
wakened for midnight polkas, pillow-groggy,
while you two toasted life. He lectured them:
your beauty, smarts, the trash can where he picked you.

Love's sacrifice. He held the gun to his head.
Your letters never mentioned that. They spread flowers
through my seasons, camphor catkins, mums,
bougainvillea wilding your yard.
"I married a man who fills our house with flowers.
I want to saturate life with life," you wrote,
teasing me for living off to the side.

The weekend I house-sat for you, messed up
and confused by simple things, I saw the picture.
All of you, smiling, strung hand in hand
across a green hillside in Austria.
Its candid happiness blazed correct and true.
Trusting nothing so complete, sick with that,
I guessed you were already, somehow, hurt.

Wearing heels as always. In the photo, at picnics,
even, I imagine, late nights in the kitchen,
sobbing again, chasing down more coffee, but clear.
Or court dates when you're in his stare again—
unannounced, he swept Number Four from school
for a shopping spree, gave Julian a birthday .22
you found under the bed. I'd return your words

if I remembered them. I can't trust myself;
the least, the commonest, harm to redeem,
and I can hardly tell the difference.

Here by the car, sober, ankles wobbly,
you can be saying We have to laugh don't we
life goes on whatever he broke my arm twice I'm a worse
hysteric now relatively sane O at least I'm still here.

The Prayer Mat

Two weeks back east, I read your letter during the news,
our F-15s stitching desert gridpoints, underground fires
out of control, the sky cored by purple smoke-jets:
"Bring me (and California) lilacs, or something lilacky.
My meditation's off. The kids that rented after us
tore out those gorgeous lilacs. They felt so unPacific.
That made me sick. I miss you and want you around the house."
Now, your candle's lilac scented light burns early
with a mockingbird's hysteria in the walnut tree.
And still, smart bombs hitting bunkers. Small war, small war.
Liquid pulse mashed blue on impact. Kneeling, you pray,
if it's prayer ("It's more like thinking"), before the candle
and its altar stash of mossed bark, acorns, kernels, stones.
State of creation, your thought coursing in I don't know
what star gas torrent of all changes, praying for balance.
More evening news. "Presidents love their video wars,
they love death so much, they make love with Christmas lights."
Then sleep. You grind your teeth, wring and chop the air.
This morning I walked past your room. Your little shrine's
blueflower smell came again. I picture you,
balancing there, behind the door, where I can't see.

On a Picture by Cézanne

There's no description in the braided stone,
the pear, the stone in the pear, the birchbark,
bread hills on the snowfall tablecloth.
The dog of work gnaws the day's short bone,
snarls a mountainside into lavender and green.
In the mind where objects vanish, almost is all.
Element of pitcher, sky, rockface; blank canvas
plastic and vast in one off-center patch.
To copy what's invisible, to improvise
a soul of things and remake solid life
into fresh anxious unlifelike form.

Ice Plant in Bloom

From where I stood at the field's immaculate edge,
walking past the open patch of land that's money bounded,
in California's flat sunlight, by suburban shadows of houses
occupied by professors, lawyers, radically affluent do-gooders,
simple casual types, plus a few plumbers, children of lettuce-pickers
and microchip princes, grandchildren of goatherds and orchard keepers
who pruned and picked apricot trees that covered what wasn't yet
block after block. Vaporized by money, by the lords and ladies of money,
in one month, on one block, three bungalows bulldozed, and the
    tanky smells
of goatherds and, before them, dirt farmers who never got enough
    water,
held momentary in the air like an album snapshot's aura,
souls of roller-rink sweethearts and sausage-makers fleeing
heaps of crusty lath, lead pipe, tiny window casements,
then new foundations poured for cozy twelve-room houses.
So what was she doing in that field among weeds and ice plant?
The yellow and pink blooms spiking around her feet like glory?
Cranking her elbow as surveyors do, to a bored watcher in the distance,
she fanned the air, clouds running low and fast behind her.

A voice seeped through the moodless sunlight
as she seemed to talk to the flowers and high weeds.
She noticed me, pointed in my direction. Accusation, election,
I could not tell, nor if it was at me myself
or the green undeveloped space she occupied,
welded into her grid by traffic noise. *Okay!*
A word for me? A go-ahead? *Okay!* Smeared by the wind
and maybe not her own voice after all. I held my place.
She would be one of the clenched ministers adrift
in bus terminals and K-Marts, carrying guns
in other parts of America, except she dressed like a casual lady of money,
running shoes, snowbird sunglasses, wristwatch like a black birthday cake.
The voice, thin and pipey, came from the boy or girl,
blond like her, who edged into view as I tracked the shot. The child,
staring down while he cried his song, slowly tread the labyrinth
of ice plant's juicy starburst flesh of leaves.
Okay! He follows the nested space between flowers that bristle at his feet,
his or hers, while the desiccated California sky so far from heaven and hell
beams down on us beings of flower, water, and flesh before we turn
    to money.
The sky kept sliding through the tips of weeds. The sky left us behind.

Red Roses

Five days later,
fuller, heavier,
blown but holding
their overripe pattern,
petals in flight
from the nowhere center . . .

Now longer, two weeks,
and redder, as if
our thought of Eden
raged inside.
What, you said. What
makes them do that?

Crouched over, shoulder
dipping toward the blooms
and their carnal thorns,
you sat up straight
when the earthquake came
that broke buildings in town,

before you bent again

to cut and trim these

to fill our largest vase.

What keeps them with us?

What do they keep?

That perfume soaks the air.

San Antonio de Padua

The soldier, the only one in sight,
stroked his skeletal, teenage moustache
and waved me through the gate.
A red-cross helicopter on its pad,
open-eyed and dense, like a housefly;
rows of tanks, half-tracks, other green vehicles;
rows of barracks with packs of new sports cars
squared off on sunny lots; basketball and tennis courts.
Road signs point to code-named spots
folded into the hills. In the Valley of the Oaks,
the first to answer Father Serra's mission bell
brought others. More came.
Soon ten thousand sheep
grazed valley-wide around the hub of vineyards,
workshops, tannery, church, and plaza.
Hot wind running in the irrigation ditches
brings smells of sage and live oak. By the Church door,
an olive tree stands taller than the facade.
Wind turns its leaves. Dried grasses stir.
A red convertible squirts down the road,
its engine whine soaked up by the wind.

I came half-hoping to find something left

from that collaboration on divinity,

the Roman God planted in our sun.

Despite the sentry's word, I stopped a half-mile short

at an unmarked Mission style building off the road.

The Mexican cleaningwoman, the only person there,

said it was, or used to be, the officers' club

(I saw a kitchenette stacked with whiskey cartons),

the rooms modeled after friars' cells,

but the real mission is down the road.

"Where is everybody?" "Oh," she said. "They're all here."

In the garden, I name what I remember.

Agave, wisteria, yucca, persimmon and fig,

"cactus" for the dozen kinds I count,

when a voice behind me says it's always water.

An old padre in coolie hat and smock

points to open trenches cut crosswise,

like the Church floorplan, up and down the garden.

"New pipes, but what good when there's no rain

for five years? We always need more water."

The cross blazed on a treetrunk two centuries ago
now lies exposed, complete, grown over in oak flesh.
A pomegranate tree, the only plant from mission days,
bears small, waxy, Baby Jesus fruit. Outside,
I trace my map to crumbling beehive ovens,
then the massive irrigation system slaves dug.
The helicopter passes. Church walls drenched in ocher,
collapsed kilns for firing tiles, tens of thousands of tiles—
fire and dirt seem to enclose, include, everything.
I know an abstract painter who, to justify his work,
says that before our early ones painted shapes
of deer, bison, hands and spears,
they painted their own bodies, as if to pull earth over us
to protect us from heaven, or to prepare us
to make images of this world. Pink wash
aureoled around the windows, turquoise window frames,
red arches painted over arches, stenciled oak leaves . . .
Inside the cool church, above the altar,
old pudgy white misshapen stars
tumble across the blue wood firmament.

Windy Hill

The Scotch broom beside the road softens the winter greens, greener now after the rainstorms, eager headstrong green with those fragrant plants bristling under the eucalyptus, though the wind is so still we can barely smell them. A few bushes straggle this far up the trail where last year, one year ago in fact, we saw rootless, astral mistletoe draining from our favorite live oak tree that cracked the depth of space behind us—we felt dizzy, fallen out of context. We remember, who was it, told us about someone who has kept herself alive with mistletoe treatments for cancer that doctors ten years ago swore would kill her in a year. Washed out in sunlight, Orion's lines run clear and pure somewhere up there in front of the galaxies, those snakes' nests. Halfway up, we're more exposed. Fewer trees, tall motionless grass. Twenty years ago, after our insomniac concierge kept us awake half the night breaking bottles in the courtyard, and after we watched the greasy Bay of Naples greening the rockwall, we took the bus and walked through the imagined ash of Pompeii. The couple caught in bed, the mother arbored over her child, the panicked dog, and those leafy wakeful faces painted or mosaicked on the walls. An army streaming from its anthill up the glassy madrone bark reminds us that when the big aftershock wobbled telephone poles several days after the earthquake, we were in the balcony, swaying in the nest while Aida sang triumph down in her tomb. Nobody panicked. At the top, we'll be just above the skyline road. The broom is still flowering somewhere near freeway ramps, by ditch water, at the edge of pastures and artichoke fields. We remember to separate them from other yellows. Not mustard flowers. Not sourgrass. Those plaster casts in the ruins remind us of the crooked groundswells in

Mathew Brady's photographs, though I think as much about the portrait of a woman holding up a stylus and wax tablet like trophies, a writer, like the woman with cancer. In the end we want a passion for form, not for efficient mastery. Plots in starlines, origins in dirt, an African princess singing above the pit where brass bells and dark woods gleam in the mud. When we finally reach the hilltop, in the still air, we'll look down on skyline, its yellow trim, and across the ridge, and beyond that to the gray ocean we can't see, where gray whales and their calves are swimming north again.

· II ·

atlantic

The Depot

When I was young, they taught us not to ask.
Accept what's there. If you want something else,
or more, don't look too shameful wanting it.
They were too right. Bituminous words,
useless rhyme, cadence, dream structures, plots
to turn life's material fact into sound—
such things helped no one, and gave nothing back.
Our mothers scrubbed sidewalks, ironed white shirts
starched upright and sure for school or Mass.
The Infant of Prague balanced his gilded globe
above the T.V. screen. On Saturdays,
we had to sit through two double features.
Between times, our fathers worked in steamy plants,
stamped dies, troweled mortar, mixed paint, broke concrete,
carpooled home to beer and shots at Mike's,
a late supper home in silence, then back to Mike's
for night baseball or cards. Our fathers taught us
we had enough. Brick homes, *Your Show of Shows*,
the mothball fleet and flaring oilworks.

I wanted just two things. Rock candy, dyed
roughcut Easter ruins, useless and real
under the drugstore counter's glass.
And the train set in someone's paneled basement,
its sweet, exact syntax of trestle, track,
village kindness with muggy lights and shops,
the switching yard, semaphores, work sheds,
and depot café where the pharmacist
drinks coffee late tonight. The waitress, Sue,
makes small talk about the pretty snow
that falls along the hills and softens the steeples.
The boxcars clack. The coffee urn hisses.
Under the counter, between stacked plates and cups,
the stink of baccalà soaks the neighborhood;
the sky, held by phonewires, sags with heat
while torn boys, squat and still on the blacktop,
skid bottlecaps from numbered square to square,
avoiding the Death Box, where motion stops,
while Sue's chapped hands unfurl above their heads.

Karloff and the Rock

FOR INJUN JOE

Weekends, pushed from small living rooms

while our parents chewed on circumstance

(bad luck's rags and rust thrown over

a mohair sofa, a gray lampshade)

we sat a fitful darkness away.

Sandwiches plumbed our coat pockets.

The bitter floor sucked at our shoes.

You said: Today's a double future,

two mummy somethings. A few rows down,

girls tucked up their legs in coats;

talcum baffled the smell of limes

that pulsed unshamed inside their skirts.

We were monkey men. Set loose

by love's distress in narrow rooms,

we whooped at their white ankle socks,

the stiff hair and frowns. You chimp-walked

the aisle, fat teeth chittering

at the screen, those skirts, yourself.

Zinc light twitched above our heads

as it did most nights on low ceilings

over all our beds. Khartoum,

Karloff, Kekrops, whoever, stirred,
cracked cellarway dust from wrappings
into a rage of wakefulness.

We ate his fright. After the show,
the winter dark outside burned bright,
so clear, so close, it made us weep
as we walked our moody shortcut home
across the scabby, weedbitten lot.
Our righteous girls went their own way.
Again we passed the limestone rock,
an altar, cut like step-up stools
we saw in kitchen catalogs,
or crumbling Sphinx where the Ragman woke.
Cars crushed their lion shadows
across the walls of redbrick homes.

Now climb (you said) the Mummy Tomb
beneath which he is gravely sunk
all these four thousand years ago,
and if it doth not budge, you bum,
you will eternal be, and free
from our curse of wanting anything.
The girls were gone. What could I know?
I climbed the stone, and when it moves,
the curse of monkey story lives
more real than flesh or figured light.
A shadow peeled from rock chased me.
I atoned. I did not run straight home.

Moving Things

My aunts mentioned her just once,
calling her my aunt, their sister,
though she wasn't. They mentioned
the vinyl recliner in the kitchen,
the "I Like Ike" poster, the Sacred Heart,
cabbage smells, sulfur, and shame.

Before jolted by the gift that called
through but never really for her,
she became unpleasantly calm.
Moments later, after she said
"I don't want this please," God's love
raced down the pulse into her look.

It was as if her things spoke back:
a table leg scraped the floor, a fork
wobbled in a drawer, knickknacks fell.
She nearly died each time it happened.
They said her mind just wasn't there,
or she wasn't in it anymore.

She sat helpless afterward,
papery when they lifted her
from vision seat to bed. The might
to move what her eye fell upon
is the image of her I keep,
her iridescent readiness.

Saturday Afternoon

"NOW YAHWEH ORDERED THAT A GREAT FISH SHOULD SWALLOW HIM."

Into my backyard's six fat squares of concrete rigged with clothesline,

Charlie the Cop swung gunnysacks convulsed with Jersey chickens.

From the open view of other yards, unfolded down the block,

neighbor women watched ours boil tub water; the barechested men,

laying out knives and cleavers, fumbled the animals into daylight,

in the middle of my world, my certain place, not stump roots

on the cold Atlantic floor of mountains I'd imagined,

one week every summer, from the hot Wildwood boardwalk.

But just then Charlie lifted me above his head, saying

"O Billy Boy you've never in your life seen this! Want it?"

The ground gone, steep drag of thinned air, chicken squawk

tingling in my ears with dim human voices. Charlie threw me in the sea.

The underplace, swallowing my heart, opened like a horn of plenty,

blood channels lit blue and red like pinball arteries, flesh-motes,

mucus, sinew, pulsing viscera bits dripping from clothesline.

Missile tracks horned across the ceiling. In the ribcage,

stooped beggars crowded, kicking spongy gouts of something;

deeper in the tunnel, toward the tail, in files winding out of sight,

shaved heads, men and women in pajamas. Spear carriers paced the walls.

Into my vaulted space came words not really words: shades, images

with a worldly shape of meaning, but beyond me, aloof and hysterical.

The silence wrapped me like a prickly woolen sleeve knit

by my women's voices, shouting, out there, unrecoverable, dense,

while their horny hands plucked and the sweaty men teased,

stuffing tacky down inside their headscarves. Inside,

blood cells combed my walls, unfinished patterns seeped through
as picturegrams that glided across the whale's belly. A still life
with ginger jar and pomegranates. A flayed, ripening Christ.
An Ohio puddler stirring pigiron mash, whose back is the same one
in Giotto's Gethsemane that stays the hand slicing off a soldier's ear.
Mercury, my heart, the sickening beautiful shiftingness of things.
Kettles steamed, tin basins quivered with guts, my dear hell's bloodglyphs
in things, in me. I'd not be whole in and of the world again.
Quills cracked when Charlie put me down. In my backyard, in my head,
women sang under a pier to the unformed sea, an unvoiced song
I'd heard inside the monster, breezing now through clotheslines.
Men scrubbed their hands at the spigot, the women sighing.
Flies left charcoal scrawls on the air and grazed old stains;
they lighted on my arms, not waiting, but constant, my familiars,
until their manic newsiness went away. Then, in that twilight,
slow, shadowless lightning bugs appeared, going on and off.

Buddy's Corner

The same fake eclairs and Communion cakes adorn D'Ambrosio's window,

now behind bars. Thirty years ago, summer wind burned inside my ears;

bits cribbed from Malory and Classics Illustrated crammed my head.

Fireplug spouts erased the air. Kids in alleys swung sticks, bottles—

once I saw them kick a black boy until blood fouled their sneakers.

"You can't hurt rubberheads," our fathers said. Adrift in old facts,

visiting home, I still ride the #2 bus into town. At Buddy's Corner,

five years in business, the glass sign's black and white hands clasping

gleam intact. Nobody enters or leaves. From behind D'Ambrosio's
   counter,

the sullen, knowing girls chew gum and watch the street. No one's buying.

When the bus jumps and swerves, my head knocks the glass, waking me

to teenage boys in high-tops and fishnet jerseys gliding alongside,

exploding eggs and tomatoes on the windows. Behind me, a girl shrieks.

A woman in cornrows snaps at the driver, "I hate nigger behavior."

Across the corner, Kim Park's Everything Store ("We Never Close")

crams the storefront where, when I was twelve, Rocco's butchershop got
   bombed

for skimming numbers bets. Peaches, tomatoes, apples, lettuce,

stacked in pristine orders. Someone, arms crossed, glares from the
   doorway.

Next stop, the Baptist church, where happy noise banned from our
   liturgy

lifted shout and response, God on the tongue, waiting there for us.

Here to there, we pass houses brickpointed smart, brass doorknockers,

potted shrubs on pavements, windowboxes blooming between white
    shutters,
then punched sheetmetal doors and windows, granite steps upended
    like logs,
brick-moss, weeds like scarecrow stuffing sprung from cracks in walls.
Old men on stoops are shouting not to make trouble, to be cool and act
    right.
Next to us, afloat between parked cars, the skinny boys stalk the bus,
sifting through tense Korean wives with grocery bags and solemn kids.
Our driver, opening the door, rolls past the church and razorwire fence.

The Sleepers

Morning light peaking on City Hall
slants juicy wedges down the stairwells
but can't seep this far underground.
A man grabs air in his fists, panting;
vapors feather from his lips.
"Well, fuck me, so then love is what?"
Sniffing, weeping almost, from urine fumes,
he and his friend, suits and ties,
Hall attorneys maybe, turning to leave.
The concourse squirms with sleepers
twisted in cardboard cribs like children
brought home late, pulling covers tighter.
"For her? She says, *Love, Jamie, what's love?*
I say I don't know what either of us is doing."
Subway cars scraping behind the tiled walls
don't wake the breathing heaps of clothes.

William Penn's chalky, sandblasted
hat and face moon above the scaffold racks
that hobble his legs. Two blocks away,
a corporate center's chrome-trimmed seagreen glass
rises higher than the Pilgrim's crown.
A woman rubs her gray head against the tiles;
the spot gleams when she totters away,
called back to our life by a boombox
thumping the corridor. Trashy, blood-clotted water,

oozing from the walls, streams across the floors
and the sleepers are drowning without a cry.
When I prowled here twenty years ago,
I thought love's better part came from books;
a word was desire's sulfur arc from breath
to instinct's needy sound, an *is* or *see*
that might take me out of this life.

A dreamy, ignorant, woozy literalist,
I wanted scenic hardware. Born here,
I'd make my dripping underground
love's pattern for a nice false heaven.
Smoke films the greasy middle air.
The harder I listen, the more Jamie's words
bleed into echoing hoots, turnstile cranks,
footsteps, whistles . . . Wet larval streaks
scribble then and now across the floors.
Penn's statue, watertight, gleams above,
custodial, second tier in the skyline.
Two bodies curl tight over steaming grates
(one foot withdraws shyly under wraps)
while heels rap past their solemn heads.
We step around the stormdrain seeps, the city
weeping in our tunnels, leaving us alone.

The Mummers

I saw them two days later.
Punk parrots strumming banjos
on the rooftops, near heaven,
glittering ranks stiff in gilt
sequins and pancake. They marched
off the edge into night space
where phonewires crossed the stars.
Sneakers drooped from the starlines.

.   .   .

"Where's the Mayor?" "Who needs him?"
Independence Hall
rolls by, buckling in the wind;
tassels bang its skirts.
Silk tents, weddingcake estates,
Betsy Ross's House.
No music. "He told his cops
to bomb their own town!"

.   .   .

The clowns, ripped and freezing, are strutting down Broad Street.
The watchers eating breakfast in high rooms look down.
The chickens strut down Broad Street, flasks in their pockets.
The high rooms, dreamed up by the dizzy clowns, approve them.
The watchers burn cork to daub their children's faces.
The chickens are lilting now from all that cheap rye.

The children, in blackface, want fried chicken for lunch.
The ripped, correct, borrowed, saved clowns dance all the way
   downtown.

   .   .   .

"One club's warehouse
went up in flames.
Costumes, makeup,
everything. So
they dressed up like
eskimos but
that New Year's was
the warmest ever."

   .   .   .

Saxophones popping frozen spitballs,
drowsy double basses, glockenspiels,
vapors rising from the scrubboard rant.
Below, men sleep in subway tunnels;
rats chew their listing cardboard cribs.
Where's our new hero of the day?
Someone bangs a Korean into a wall
for selling pink carnations on New Year's Day.

   .   .   .

When the marchers go
off the edge of rooftops,
the music doesn't stop
inside my head. Winter

stops, the subway roars,
cracking towers flare
behind the roofs. Under
me the sidewalk quakes.

Self-Portrait

An idling car out front. Phone wires,
doo-wop chimes, sycamore bark.
Nobody home to shut the lights
or tip the string band in the alley.
Sobs from the picture tube, my other language
looning in the screen: Milton Berle in drag,
his sweet elastic jackass face and painted lips.
But someone's upstairs now, drunk or weepy,
bedridden since this dream time started,
the voice calling through the aluminum air
around Uncle Miltie's skirts, on Walnut Street,
a springtime afternoon creased with poplar seeds
that film the pavement outside the Eakins shrine,
his *Gross Clinic*, Marsyas on the workbench,
no Apollo, the mother cringing from the open flesh

> though *The Actress*, in Philadelphia, is truer, more sensuous, for
> its canny and stubborn refusal to illustrate (*Don't illustrate existence,*
> *make an image*) but Eakins is still too fond of anecdote to be mod-
> ern in a way we feel along our nerves. Form for me is the
> amazed failure of completed feeling. Fury and love toil happily
> there, changing. Even the classic Cézanne had no method, he
> was always improvising.

Sister Joseph's voice buzzes the high sash windows,
the Picture Study pamphlet, the stifling air,
God in colors of *The Angelus*,
poem emergent in a broken alien idiom

spoken by what Henry James, our official European, revisiting
New York in his Master years, referred to as "the launched pop-
ulations," insisting that the language bound to evolve from that
usage would be singular, distinct, and not English.

Banjo rant, streetcorner songs,

not rote or schoolroom ceremony.

The peasants pause at their work,

haystacks dust their hair and food,

voices gathering upstairs now,

a man and woman cry to each other,

words suffering to fall clear

may never fall clear in words.

But everyone's up there, out there

hanging wash in steerage,

on their way to this.

22nd Street

The grass that winter killed was already half-gone with blight or smog. You thought it was funny, that we called our dingy pavement moss "grass." The stiff weeds rising from the cracks in concrete were grass, too. Your singing was not nature, it made up for the blight and death and didn't have seasons. Fifties' ballads, early Elvis, Peggy Lee teasers, "Little Tommy Tucker" and "Kyrie Eleison." I listened from my room upstairs on spring days, when the grass was growing and your voice lifted and slid up over the street noise. Squirming on your front steps, watching sparrows bop around the sewer grates, you couldn't wait to get going and be a teen. Your songs took me out of my books but became part of them, like initial illustrations, the gildered red vine of your voice separating words and binding them. "Nature hammers us, her children," my poet says, "with sober promises unmade or betrayed." What are we meant for? Making our First Communion, I was pious and hortatory, you were shy and bounced your petticoats. What could we have known? A story gets old, we say, but the irreducible facts don't change. Quit business school, the demo tapes, a husband, in and out of shelters or recovery units, a husband again, and in the end the car wreck. Witness or testimony? I don't know my own reason. This feels like another life. Whatever I say, you're not in these words. From your distance, out of nature, not singing.

St. Monica's at 17th & Ritner

The squatters keep arriving, at all hours,
    while sunshine drains yellow under ginkgo trees
and the bleachy sycamores enlarge toward dark.
    Singly, paired up, they come to nest inside
where it's warm. Mica spangles the churchstones,
    the fizzling stained glass shot by drumtapped light
from cooking fires among the pews. For days,
    I've watched them come, as if called, homing, sure
of whatever sign or need that brings them here.
    Redbrick housefronts stricken by fall light.
Buicks double-parked. The hardware store's
    seed packets, midget turf loaves, redwood planters.
I've seen bindlestiffs climb the steps and knock;
    salesmen with sample cases, and leather kids
dragging shopping carts scribbled with kindling.
    I dream the old sounds our rivers make,
the Schuylkill slit by hissing sculls or torched
    by refinery flares. O dem golden slippers.
The Delaware's whiskey boats, the Fourth's fireworks.
    At least they move. Here things stop.
The clouds are like a green lake soaked by sun.
    Clouds nothing like a lake. What god
    lives with us in words? What word suffices?

. . .

Across from the church,
the pork-butcher's signs
recruit nuns and priests.
He stocks giveaway glow-
in-the-dark rosaries.
Hoots, barking dogs, too,
behind the high crazed glass.
Once inside, nobody leaves.
Newcomers bring clothes,
canned food, paper,
party horns and sugar.
Furia's Funeral Home,
just across the street,
where they laid out Jimmy T.,
"Helicopter Gunner:
1965."
("Gunner where ?")
The hardware store's shaggy bunting draped on rakes and hoes says
NUKE DUNE COONS VOTE OUR FRANK. Mr. Rizzo dropped
dead while campaigning for a third mayoral term, who twenty years
ago, as Police Commissioner, rousted Panther headquarters at 3 A.M.,
stripped the males and lined them up along the street, the New World
Porch, for the press photographers' front page. At a party a few weeks
later, a guy wearing a dashiki and smoking plenty dope, a cop, explained
to me how he stood by Commissioner Frank no matter what, because he
didn't send men into a gun fight, he said "Follow me." (Voted out of
office, Frank became a popular radio talk show host.)

. . .

Nobody knows how it started, what relics
    drew pilgrims from Fishtown, Camden, and Manayunk,
to throw out the priests, sack the rectory,
    build excelsior cribs in chancel and transept.
We keep clear of the walls and fence aglitter
    with broken bottles. Leaves gum the pavement,
traffic lights leaping from busted sockets.
    Some nights the new believers dance or strut,
campfire shadows twitch across the high windows
    like Malaysian puppets. I imagine
manic shades chased across the Stations.
    Pilate's stone bowl and the bloody pillar.
I smell pew varnish smoking, and incense.
    The dancing shades of those worshipers
are the soul in ecstasy, before body shrieked.
    I hear them chanting rumdumb sacrifice
of dogs and cats they butcher on the stones:
    O darling Christ and Saviour
How much killing in Your name without You?
    How many more good wars?

．　．　．

Thugs, addicts, housewives,
the card store lady, kids
(local good kids),
the loudmouth Calabrese
who opened "Bella Bagel"
and made out like a bandit,
safe inside St. Monica's,
at prayer, joyful
in their new city.
We're safe in our cities.
The President is safe.
The President has been shot.
Swayback river rats
slide down the basement transoms.
On marble floors (just where
I prayed to my father's soul)
they're rolling rat bones, feathers,
squat on doghide mats,
hissing at the fire god.
The mystery is we suffer
without deliverance,
and love suffers what's real.

. . .

Last night, neighborhood boys streamed from alleys,
    wearing Nixon masks, boots, and long-nosed codpieces.
The eggs they splashed against the nervous windows
    gave the glass a slimed, bleary radiance.
Maytime this year, our boys and girls in white,
    as I was, won't pass through the tall bronze doors
after they've walked around the walls three times,
    two by two, silent, lifting heel and toe.

· III ·

Reading Ovid

"Contrition, rhyme, eyelashes, leaders beggaring imagination . . ."
Foul water delirium. Caesar's a junkyard dog
turned on his scrapmetal master, singing master.
A Black Sea resort, bad food, mosquitoes, no wine,
cornpone democracy that makes beggars citizens. Love baits,
teases, poontang scripts, favors he taught girls to beg
from potbellied industrialists, nothing helps now.
Canny technologue Daedalus warned his febrile son
to stay a middle course, not burn up or belly down.
Daedalus was right. Sweats and hungers into words,
love's appetite and casual anarchy,
that's no proper world. Poetry wants too much.
His pasty sun sets on bramble farms and clay fields.
Washed up, he needs new subjects, or change of heart.
He has materials: frequent night raids, poison arrows
he's learning to shoot, a wife back home, animal pictures
tortured on her loom. And Augustus, cold war strategist,
peeping at every bedroom window but his own.

The boonies mock a city's fine scales of grit, girls,

sidewalk saxophonists, graffiti, cops, hot food and sugar . . .

You can't say a Senator, or his wife, screws dogs

and expect people to appreciate your style.

Well-bred ironies make you famous and employed.

A poem a day, stale myths, elegiac whining,

whatever cuts contrition's briny taste.

His new friends don't care about his rhymes

and will never understand his Latin. Shipped back home,

these new poems get him nowhere with state bureaucrats.

He's picking up the phlegmy local language;

he pretends to make small talk with street vendors.

He's learning to be of use. Bowlegged, stalking the walls,

helmet raked cockeyed on his heavy, graying head,

when looters cross the plain to storm the so-called town,

he stands with the defenders, crowing his new words,

protecting the only piece of writing he can claim:

stone gardens, malarial fields, trees he can't even name.

Note

"Windy Hill" and "22nd Street" derive from two poems by Giacomo Leopardi, *"La ginestra"* and *"A Silvia."* Death Box is a Philadelphia street game in which players move bottlecaps through a series of numbered squares arranged around a large central square called the Death Box; landing in the Death Box, a player must wait several turns before moving again. In "Saturday Afternoon," the Ohio puddler is a figure in a water-color by Joseph Stella, the still life refers to a painting by Cézanne, and the Giotto image is part of the fresco cycle in the Scrovegni Chapel. In "Self-Portrait," the Eakins shrine is the small exhibition gallery in the Jefferson Medical School in Philadelphia where "The Gross Clinic" and other paintings are on permanent display. "Reading Ovid" was occasioned by David R. Slavitt's translation *Ovid's Poetry of Exile,* and its language owes something to the spirit of that work.